YORK NOTES

A Taste of Honey

Shelagh Delaney

Note by Bernadette Dyer

 Longman   York Press

Bernadette Dyer is hereby identified as author of this work in accordance with Section 77 of the Copyright, Designs and Patents Act 1988

YORK PRESS
322 Old Brompton Road, London SW5 9JH

PEARSON EDUCATION LIMITED
Edinburgh Gate, Harlow,
Essex CM20 2JE, United Kingdom
Associated companies, branches and representatives throughout the world

First published 1999
10 9 8 7 6 5 4 3

ISBN 978-0-582-38229-9

Designed by Vicki Pacey
Illustrated by Judy Stevens
Phototypeset by Gem Graphics, Trenance, Mawgan Porth, Cornwall
Colour reproduction and film output by Spectrum Colour
Printed in China (EPC/03)

C ONTENTS

PREFACE

York Notes are designed to give you a broader perspective on works of literature studied at GCSE and equivalent levels. We have carried out extensive research into the needs of the modern literature student prior to publishing this new edition. Our research showed that no existing series fully met students' requirements. Rather than present a single authoritative approach, we have provided alternative viewpoints, empowering students to reach their own interpretations of the text. York Notes provide a close examination of the work and include biographical and historical background, summaries, glossaries, analyses of characters, themes, structure and language, cultural connections and literary terms.

If you look at the Contents page you will see the structure for the series. However, there's no need to read from the beginning to the end as you would with a novel, play, poem or short story. Use the Notes in the way that suits you. Our aim is to help you with your understanding of the work, not to dictate how you should learn.

York Notes are written by English teachers and examiners, with an expert knowledge of the subject. They show you how to succeed in coursework and examination assignments, guiding you through the text and offering practical advice. Questions and comments will extend, test and reinforce your knowledge. Attractive colour design and illustrations improve clarity and understanding, making these Notes easy to use and handy for quick reference.

York Notes are ideal for:
• Essay writing
• Exam preparation
• Class discussion

The author of this Note, Bernadette Dyer, has an MA and BA in English from the University of Manchester. She is a senior examiner and senior moderator in English and English Literature for a major GCSE board. Formerly Head of English at Newall Green High School, Manchester, she now teaches English in a sixth form college. The text used in this Note is the Heinemann Plays edition of *A Taste of Honey* by Shelagh Delaney (Heinemann, 1992).

Health Warning: This study guide will enhance your understanding, but should not replace the reading of the original text and/or study in class.

PART ONE

INTRODUCTION

HOW TO STUDY A PLAY

You have bought this book because you wanted to study a play on your own. This may supplement classwork.

- Drama is a special 'kind' of writing (the technical term is 'genre') because it needs a performance in the theatre to arrive at a full interpretation of its meaning. When reading a play you have to imagine how it should be performed; the words alone will not be sufficient. Think of gestures and movements.

- Drama is always about conflict of some sort (it may be below the surface). Identify the conflicts in the play and you will be close to identifying the large ideas or themes which bind all the parts together.

- Make careful notes on themes, characters, plot and any sub-plots of the play.

- Playwrights find non-realistic ways of allowing an audience to see into the minds and motives of their characters. The 'soliloquy', in which a character speaks directly to the audience, is one such device. Does the play you are studying have any such passages?

- Which characters do you like or dislike in the play? Why? Do your sympathies change as you see more of these characters?

- Think of the playwright writing the play. Why were these particular arrangements of events, these particular sets of characters and these particular speeches chosen?

Shelagh Delaney wrote the script for *A Taste of Honey* in the late 1950s when she was just eighteen years old. Born in 1939, she was reared and educated in Salford, Lancashire in north-west Britain. She left school at sixteen and had a series of jobs which included shop assistant and usherette but she was always interested in writing. Disappointed with the drama of the 1950s which largely tended to reflect upper-class life, Shelagh Delaney felt she could write something better which would realistically portray the lives of characters from the working class. She therefore turned a novel she was writing into a play, *A Taste of Honey*, and sent it off to Joan Littlewood who ran one of London's more inventive theatre companies.

Joan Littlewood was impressed with the vitality and wisdom of the work and immediately began to produce the play, making some additions and alterations. She encouraged much improvisation, based on the original script and characters but including new scenes and situations. The final script was similar to the original but Peter was now less of a straightforward, pleasant character and the play's ending no longer had Jo sent off to hospital to have her baby.

A Taste of Honey became an international success.

A Taste of Honey opened at the Theatre Royal, London, in 1958 and was so successful it moved to the West End in 1959. Critics were impressed with the play's originality, directness and humour. When the play was performed in New York in 1960, Walter Kerr wrote in the *New York Herald Tribune* 'It leaves you breathless'. Like so many other critics, Kerr admired the fast-moving **dialogue** (see Literary Terms) and humour of the play as did Robert Hatch in *Horizon* who described *A Taste of Honey* as 'a witty tragedy'.

Shelagh Delaney went on to write a second play, *The Lion in Love* (1960) which had a more complex plot than the first play but did not receive the same level of critical acclaim. Apart from a short story collection, *Sweetly Sings the Donkey* (1963), most of Shelagh Delaney's work since has been as a scriptwriter for film and television.

One of her more well-known screenplays was *Charley Bubbles* (1968) starring Albert Finney, the story of a novelist who tries unsuccessfully to return to his northern, working-class life. Another of Shelagh Delaney's screenplays which might present a valuable insight into life in the 1950s is *Dance with a Stranger* (1982), which retells the story of Ruth Ellis, the last woman to be executed in England.

The conflict between parent and child is a central theme in the play.

A Taste of Honey was praised for its strikingly authentic portraits of working-class people in the 1950s. For many, the play was memorable because it seemed Shelagh Delaney was writing from first-hand experience of working-class life in a northern, industrial city. The central **character** (see Literary Terms) is Jo who is still at school when the play opens and is locked into generational conflict with her mother, Helen, as the two struggle to cope with financial hardship and insecurity of industrial life. In contrast with the popular plays of the time, *A Taste of Honey* dealt with contemporary issues which were considered to be quite shocking. Jo is a teenager who becomes pregnant after a brief interracial love affair with a sailor and then goes on to share her home with a homosexual. Her mother is a divorced semi-prostitute with a particular fondness for alcohol. As the characters live out their lives struggling against financial hardship and personal insecurities within a deprived, industrial setting, we gain an insight into the attitudes of ordinary people, including racist, sexist and homophobic views.

However, the lives of the central **characters** (see Literary Terms) are not wholly burdened by the hardships of life, for each one experiences some happiness and love, their own 'taste of honey'. Jo has a short-lived love affair with a sailor and also derives comfort and affection from her friendship with Geof. Meanwhile Helen is obviously happy to marry Peter and enjoy some financial security while the marriage lasts. In fact, despite the hardships and apparent conflicts between the characters, Shelagh Delaney's play does convey a sense of hope. The play does not provide easy solutions to problems but it does celebrate the characters' enthusiasm for life.

Helen and Jo both attract male admirers.

All the characters in the play engage in lively and realistic **dialogue** (see Literary Terms), a feature which attracted considerable critical acclaim. The language used is **colloquial** (see Literary Terms) but contains few indications of a northern working-class dialect. In part this may have been because Shelagh Delaney wished to present the characters as articulate and intelligent individuals who were wise as well as comical and so she wrote dialogue which reflected the way ordinary people she knew, spoke. The characters presented are imperfect for they can be angry, changeable, selfish, coarse and sometimes racist and prejudiced. Similarly, these same characters can be caring and considerate. Throughout the play the characters speak like real people and Shelagh Delaney thus conveys a convincing portrait of working-class people in the 1950s.

SETTING

The action of the play takes place within a flat and on the street outside. The flat is a run-down, rented 'maisonette' located in a deprived part of industrial Manchester. It overlooks a gasworks and is close to a canal, a slaughterhouse and a cemetery. The poverty of the area is conveyed through descriptions of dirt, tenements and poor, undernourished, filthy children. Similarly, references to prostitution and theft convey a forceful image of the social deprivation of the area.

Housing was scarce in the post–war Britain of the 1950s.

The flat is draughty, damp, dirty and poorly equipped. The roof leaks into rooms lit by unshaded light bulbs. The fire fails to work and the cooker is faulty. It is sparsely furnished with an uncomfortable sofa, a chair and bed. There is a shared bathroom at the end of a corridor which is unclean and, according to Peter, is infested with cockroaches. The undesirable conditions are worsened by Jo and Helen's untidiness and lack of attention to hygiene. Throughout the play the noise of local children singing and playing on the streets echoes in the background.

PART TWO

SUMMARIES

GENERAL SUMMARY

Act I Scene 1
The play is set in a cheerless flat in a poor part of Manchester close to a gasworks and slaughterhouse. When the first scene opens the two central **characters** (see Literary Terms) enter the flat carrying their baggage. Helen is complaining of a heavy cold as her daughter Jo complains about the condition of the flat.

Notice the quick moving, often witty dialogue between Helen and Jo.
The mother and daughter relationship is strained as each criticises the other's behaviour. As Jo attempts to make the place more comfortable, Helen drinks whisky and we learn that the two women have had many different homes which resulted in a disrupted education for Jo who is now in her final term at school. When Jo mentions her future, Helen recalls her past when she used to sing in pubs. Helen discovers some of Jo's drawings and is impressed by Jo's ability and talks about sending her to Art School. Jo is unresponsive and complains again about having to move around so much. Just as Jo is about to go to the communal bathroom for a bath Peter Smith, an admirer of Helen, arrives. Helen is curious to know how Peter managed to trace her and he is surprised to discover she has a teenage daughter. He begins to flirt with Helen and asks her to consider marrying him. Meanwhile Jo is ignored and made to feel unwelcome. Eventually Peter agrees to leave when Helen refuses to go out for a drink because of her heavy cold. The scene ends as mother and daughter retire to bed and Jo expresses her fear of the dark.

Act I Scene 2
This scene contains a number of shorter scenes. It begins with Jo meeting her boyfriend, a black naval officer referred to as Boy. He offers to marry Jo when he is next on leave, in six months time, and gives her a

ring which she wears on a ribbon around her neck. It is obvious the couple have not known each other for long and it is clear that the sailor does not want to spend all his time with Jo. After arranging a meeting the next day Boy leaves and Jo enters the next part of the scene in a dreamy and happy mood. Jo relates some of the details about her boyfriend to Helen but does not mention their intention to marry. The two women chat about a number of topics including contemporary films, a fortune teller and the reasons why Helen's marriage broke up. Helen then announces her intention to marry Peter Smith, news which Jo does not receive happily.

Notice the resentment shown by Jo towards Peter.

Shortly after, Peter arrives carrying flowers for Helen and chocolates for Jo. There is a hostile exchange between Jo and Peter which takes place as Helen prepares to leave. Jo fires a series of questions at Peter and tries to deter him from marrying Helen. The couple finally depart to celebrate finding a house and leave Jo distressed and alone in the flat. A while later, in the next part of this scene, Jo is joined by her boyfriend from whom she seeks some comfort and company. Although the couple talk about their love for each other, it is apparent that the sailor will probably not actually return to marry Jo. This does not prevent Jo from persuading the sailor to stay with her over Christmas. In the final part of this scene Jo has left school and is about to begin work. Helen is busy dressing for her wedding but reacts angrily when she notices Jo's wedding ring and discovers Jo has promised to marry her sailor boyfriend. As Helen resumes her preparations Jo asks questions about her father and learns he was slightly 'retarded'. Although Jo is obviously worried by this information Helen speaks affectionately about the man who she loved even though at the time she was married to someone else who eventually divorced her for adultery. The scene concludes as Helen exits to become Peter's wife leaving Jo alone again to fend for herself.

Act II Scene 1 The second act begins late one summer evening during the following year as Jo returns to the same flat from a fair. Jo is accompanied by Geoffrey Ingram who she invites to stay in the flat after admitting that she is pregnant by her sailor boyfriend. The major part of the scene describes the developing friendship between Jo and Geof who is homosexual and provides her with practical support and affection. Geof is an art student who tries to encourage Jo to make the necessary preparations for her child by making baby clothes, getting a wicker cradle and buying a book called

Note Geof's consideration and tolerance.

Looking after Baby. In contrast Jo complains that she does not want to be a mother. At one point Geof tries to kiss Jo passionately and asks her to marry him. When Jo refuses him and suggests she might be better leaving he states he would rather be dead than away from her.

Towards the close of the scene Helen pays a visit as she has learned of Jo's pregnancy. Immediately an argument develops and both Jo and Geof are criticised or insulted by Helen. When they calm down Geof is instructed to make tea as Helen declares her intention to help by leaving some money. However, the scene becomes unpleasant once more when Peter appears, drunk and abusive, particularly towards Geof. Peter is verbally aggressive towards Jo and also toward Helen, indicating that he is regretting his marriage to her. He takes back the money Helen has left and contradicts much of what Helen earlier stated. When Helen and Peter finally exit harmony is restored and the scene ends with Geof and Jo dancing.

Act II Scene 2 Some months later Jo and Geof are still together as Jo enters the final stage of her pregnancy. While Geof cleans the flat, the two chat and laugh about a range of topics including Jo's fears that the baby will be 'simple-minded' like her father. Geof's attempt to encourage Jo to practise nursing a baby, by giving her a life-sized doll, upsets her because the doll is the wrong colour.

Decide whether Helen returns because of Jo's situation or because of her own marriage breakdown.

Unannounced, Helen enters loaded with luggage declaring her intention to care for Jo once more. When Geof is forced to leave the flat briefly, Helen eventually admits Peter has left her for another woman. As Jo rests Geof returns and is mocked and bullied by Helen until she succeeds in compelling him to depart. When Jo tells Helen her baby's father is black, Helen is shocked and goes out of the flat saying she needs a drink. The scene ends with Jo, alone in the flat and unaware that Geof has left, reciting a nursery rhyme.

DETAILED SUMMARIES

ACT I

SCENE 1   Throughout the play music is played as **characters** (see Literary Terms) enter and exit. As this first scene begins the stage directions tell us that there is jazz music playing as Helen and her teenage daughter Jo enter carrying luggage. The setting is a badly equipped flat, described by Jo as a 'ruin', which is part of a lodging house located near a river in a poor area of Manchester. The first words spoken by mother and daughter indicate disagreement between them which is in fact a common feature of their relationship throughout the play. Helen is described as a semi-whore and Jo refers to Helen's 'immoral earnings' which suggests that Helen gains money through her men friends.

What reasons does Helen give for drinking heavily?

Helen's first demand is for a glass for her whisky, which she seems to enjoy drinking regularly. When Jo complains of the lack of heating Helen offers her a glass of whisky too, knowing Jo obviously disapproves.

Jo attempts to shade the exposed light bulb using a scarf and then notices that the roof is leaking. Although Helen admits the flat is a bit of a mess Jo continues to criticise her mother for rushing into decisions. It is at this point that we learn the women have had to move frequently. Next, Jo explores the kitchen to boil water for coffee while Helen continues to complain about her cold symptoms. The two talk about men and Helen's many boyfriends. Jo has never had a boyfriend although she expressed interest in one of Helen's 'fancy men'.

At times it seems that Jo and Helen are talking to themselves not each other.

When Jo complains about the river's smell there is a brief focus on the flat's location. Its proximity to the slaughterhouse suggests there are likely to be further unpleasant smells. Significantly, there is a cemetery close by which prompts thoughts of death and decay, themes which run through the play.

Jo unpacks some flower bulbs which she tells Helen she took from 'The Park'. When Jo talks of her intention to leave school at Christmas, Helen is prompted to talk fondly about her first job singing in a pub on Whit Lane. This results in a bitter exchange as Jo accuses Helen of ruining her life and declares her intention to never marry. The conversation topic is then swiftly changed as Jo describes her dream about police finding Helen buried under a rosebush. Helen reacts by making a light-hearted comment that dead bodies should be used to make manure. When Helen finds some of Jo's drawings she is impressed by Jo's ability and offers to pay to send her to an art school. It is here we learn that their many moves have disrupted Jo's education.

What reason is suggested by Jo to explain why they left the previous place?

The two women continue to argue and bicker at each other until Peter Smith, a car salesman, enters. It is obvious that Helen is shocked by his appearance and Jo surmises that he was probably the reason why they had moved away from their previous home. Helen does not seem overjoyed to see Peter but is curious to discover how he found their new flat. Although he is surprised to find Helen has a daughter it does not stop him displaying his obvious sexual attraction to Helen. He is eager to spend time alone with Helen and is therefore dismissive of Jo. When Peter questions Helen's reasons for moving to such a bad district, she makes several comments about giving up work and going 'free lance' which suggest she wants to break ties with her past. Peter flirts with Helen and tries to persuade her to go for a drink. When he asks Helen to marry him she does not take him seriously reminding him that she is old enough to be his mother. Peter makes it clear he likes older women. He frequently sings lines from popular songs in an attempt to convince Helen she should marry him and boasts of his good looks and prospects.

When Jo brings in the coffee she has made, both Helen and Peter are unfriendly towards her. Jo is able to respond to their comments with sarcasm and quick-witted answers. Helen maintains that Jo is jealous because she does not like to see Helen being affectionate which instantly prompts Jo to be critical of Helen's failure to be an affectionate mother. Peter is not perturbed by Jo's comments or rude interruptions as he continues flirting with Helen, offering her an engagement ring and telling her a rude story. In an effort to gain attention Jo comments on Peter's cigar. This prompts Peter to suggest that Jo should go to her real father. When told her real father is dead he merely mutters 'too bad' and resumes his vulgar story. As Jo persists with comments about the cigar, Peter makes a coarse racist remark and remains unperturbed that her mother is 'a devil with the men'. As soon as Peter is persuaded to leave Helen prepares to go to bed leaving the unpacking until the next day. Helen compares the bed they share to a coffin.

The mention of a coffin is just one of many references made to death throughout the play.

Jo refers to other occasions in the past when she was obviously made to feel unwelcome because of Helen's men friends, which might explain why she was so hostile towards Peter Smith. She also talks of her fear of the darkness in houses which contrasts with Helen's view of darkness as something which disguises the truth.

COMMENT

Helen and Jo are the main **characters** (see Literary Terms) in the play and the nature of their parent and child relationship is a central theme. The language they use to refer to each other often reflects their feelings towards one another. Jo calls her mother 'Helen' which might suggest a lack of respect or simply that she sees herself as Helen's equal. Similarly, although Helen does address her daughter by name she also regularly refers to her in the third person as 'she', which creates a sense of emotional distance.

Conversations between the mother and daughter are made up of short, sharp comments as they frequently disagree and criticise each other. The **dialogue** (see Literary Terms) moves quickly from one topic to another as various aspects of their past and present lives are described. There appears to be a lack of affection between the two as both point out the other's faults and inadequacies, but there are also some positive aspects to their relationship.

GLOSSARY   **shilling in the slot affairs** gas meters which accept the old shilling, worth five pence in decimal currency

redeeming feature good qualities to make up for weaknesses or faults

aspidistra large, leafy plant

tenements buildings divided into dwellings for families

renege to go back on

slouch an idle person

the cat's been on the strawberries this is something of an insult which refers to a prostitute, 'a cat' and alcohol abuse

TEST YOURSELF (ACT I SCENE 1)

A *Identify the speaker.*

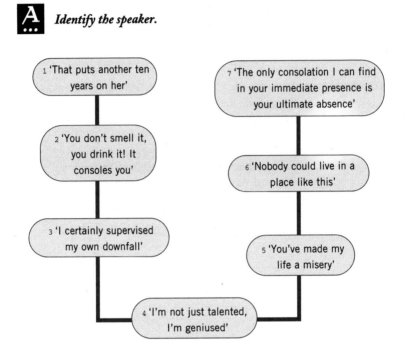

1 'That puts another ten years on her'

2 'You don't smell it, you drink it! It consoles you'

3 'I certainly supervised my own downfall'

4 'I'm not just talented, I'm geniused'

5 'You've made my life a misery'

6 'Nobody could live in a place like this'

7 'The only consolation I can find in your immediate presence is your ultimate absence'

Check your answers on page 61.

B *Consider these issues.*

a The humour in many of the comments which pass between the characters.

b How Helen and Jo frequently disagree.

c The possible effects of Helen's liking for alcohol.

d Jo's attitude towards her schooling.

e Whether Helen is a caring mother.

f Peter's reluctance to use Helen's name.

g The number of times Peter uses lines from popular songs.

h The social deprivation of the location.

ACT I

SCENE 2

How does Helen react at the end of the play when she learns that the father of Jo's baby is black?

The first part of this scene takes place on the street outside the flat as Jo is talking with her boyfriend, a black sailor. It occurs a week before Jo leaves school to work part-time in a bar, just as her mother did years earlier. The theme of darkness is continued from the previous scene with the sailor echoing Helen's preference for the dark. When the sailor kisses Jo he realises that she really does not care about being kissed in public and is so happy she tells him she loves him. Like her mother in the previous scene, Jo receives a marriage proposal from the sailor. The sailor offers Jo an engagement ring and asks her about Helen's likely reaction to his colour. Jo defends her mother declaring that Helen is not prejudiced against colour but suggests she wears the ring on a ribbon around her neck as it is too big.

When the sailor empties his pockets, it is noted that he carries a toy car, which might be viewed as a way of linking him with Peter the car salesman. Although the sailor talks about not having much time with Jo he also jokes about being 'trapped' into marriage and calls Jo a 'shameless woman' as well as making comments about

women never having 'young minds' which reminds us of
the type of comments Peter makes about women. The
sailor then makes a reference to the title when he
addresses Jo as 'Honey'. He does not meet Jo that
evening because he had planned an evening out with
the 'lads' all of which raises questions about how
committed he is to Jo and the idea of marriage.
However, Jo does not appear to be too worried about
her boyfriend's imminent departure even when her
romantic notions about his black ancestry are deflated
as she learns that his family were from Cardiff, in
Wales rather than Africa.

Arranging to meet the next day, the couple kiss and
part, each talking of dreams. Jo dances dreamily into
the next part of the scene to join Helen who is reading
a newspaper. Helen immediately senses Jo's mood and
enjoys finding out about her boyfriend, focusing
particularly on the fact that he has long legs and is a
nurse. The conversation topic is switched by Jo to the

*Note how Jo and
Helen have
opposing views
about marital
infidelity.*

films being screened. Helen's comments here are
particularly revealing as she expresses her disapproval of
the contemporary theatre, cinema and advertising. Jo
remarks she would rather be a prostitute than go into
the film industry for, in her opinion, it is a more
'honest' profession. Once again Jo changes the direction
of the conversation and begins to ask Helen further
questions about her childhood and Helen's husband
who had ended their marriage when he discovered
Helen was pregnant by Jo's father. Helen blames Jo for
the break-up of her marriage. As the conversation topic
changes to destiny, Helen states her realistic view of life
that individuals have to work and take charge of their

*Notice how
Helen's views of
life and destiny
are linked to the
image of a car.*

own destiny. **Ironically** (see Literary Terms), she
conjures up an amusing image of a drunken driver
steering a path through life just as she announces she is
going to marry Peter Smith.

Jo is instantly critical of her mother, arguing that Helen is too old to marry. Although we are not given Helen's precise age it seems she is roughly forty years of age. When Peter enters, carrying chocolates for Jo and flowers for Helen, Jo greets him mockingly as 'Daddy' and persists in making further rude comments about Helen's age and figure. When Helen leaves the room Jo physically attacks Peter, childishly demanding that he leaves her and Helen alone. Helen calms Jo, explaining that they are going away celebrating because Peter has found a new, white house. While Helen changes Peter willingly answers Jo's most probing personal questions about his family and how he lost an eye during the war. Peter shows Jo a photograph of the house and lets her see other photographs in his wallet of his former girlfriends. She even tries to draw Peter's opinion about her looks and repeatedly questions his motives for marrying Helen. Once more, Peter declares his preference for older women and sings about love. Off-stage Helen can also be heard singing. When Helen is finally ready he compliments her appearance and playfully tries on her hat. Helen's failure to be amused by his antics prompts him to complain about her lack of a sense of humour and perhaps hints at the differences between the two which will ultimately lead to separation.

Examine Peter's responses to Jo's questions and consider what they reveal about him and his attitudes to women.

Helen complains about books Jo has left lying around the flat including the Bible which Jo recommends Helen should read. The number of biblical references Jo makes during the play suggest that this is not just an idle comment. Peter sneers at Jo's disapproval of their excessive behaviour. When Jo challenges Helen once more about her reasons for marrying Peter, her short reply suggests the money in his wallet attracts her, whereas Jo knows the wallet also contains pictures of other women. It is noticeable that Helen does not mention love whenever she talks of marriage.

Despite her complaints about being left alone when she is hungry and needs money, Jo is ignored by Helen who is mainly concerned about keeping Peter from being upset, not about her role as a mother. As the happy couple depart for an unstated period of time, Peter expresses relief about leaving the area which he describes as a 'black hole of Calcutta', a term used to describe very overcrowded, dark places.

Note Jo says she would rather go to her own funeral than be Helen's bridesmaid.

Jo watches the couple depart and then lies on the bed and cries. Music plays and her sailor boyfriend appears. Noticing she has been crying he offers to make her a milky drink, commenting upon how he hates the dirty area. Like Peter, he believes it's the 'dirtiest place' he has ever seen. He had seen Helen and Peter departing and comments upon how young Helen looked. When questioned by Jo her boyfriend states clearly that Jo is not like her mother. He makes it very clear that he has 'dishonourable intentions' towards Jo and playfully compares himself to Othello, Shakespeare's black prince who murdered Desdemona. These comments draw attention to his skin colour and indicate that he is probably well-read. Despite the engagement ring there are repeated references to the fact that the two of them may never see each other again, but this does not stop Jo encouraging the sailor to stay with her over Christmas. Interestingly, it is the sailor who echoes Jo's words from the earlier scene when he tells her that, although he doesn't know the reason why, he loves her.

Consider carefully why Helen is so opposed to the idea of Jo getting married young.

As the scene fades out wedding bells sound while Helen enters to prepare for her wedding day. Jo now has a heavy cold and does not share Helen's enthusiasm. When Helen comments about the sunshine, Jo makes a gloomy reference to death. **Ironically** (see Literary Terms), Helen reacts angrily when she discovers Jo's wedding ring, accusing her of being too young and silly for marriage. When Helen's anger subsides she urges Jo not to wed too young but to learn from her mother's mistakes. It does seem strange that Helen should object so strongly to the idea of Jo entering marriage when she is just about to be married for the second time in her life. The two briefly become closer as Jo warns her mother not to drink so heavily and compliments her for looking 'marvellous,

Note the references   considering'. Helen jokes about heaven and hell until Jo
made at this point   once again asks about her father. Helen reveals that he
to heaven and the   was 'retarded' which instantly alarms Jo, prompting her
devil.   to ask whether madness can be inherited. Helen gives a fuller description of the man she remembers with obvious affection. The scene is concluded on a friendly note as Jo wishes her mother 'Good luck' as she leaves to marry Peter accompanied by the sound of 'Here comes the Bride' played on a cornet.

COMMENT   In Britain in the 1950s interracial relationships and marriage were frowned upon by many people. In the **context** (see Literary Terms) of the time Shelagh Delaney's introduction of Jo's black boyfriend would, therefore, have been quite controversial. It is interesting to notice how he questions Jo about her mother's reaction to him, which probably indicates that he anticipates disapproval because he is 'a coloured boy'.

It is also important to note that Jo's boyfriend is not given a name at this stage but is simply referred to as 'Boy'. Jo does not acknowledge him as 'Jimmie' until Act II Scene 2.

It is worth comparing the two men, Peter and the sailor, and their obvious sexual attraction to Helen and

Note the sailor's comment about women's minds.

Jo. Both propose marriage and offer gifts to convince the females of their interest yet it is clear that both are also interested in other women. Significantly, Peter appears to have a greater level of commitment to Helen in that he actually does marry her and finds them a house, whereas the sailor talks only in vague terms about the future.

Notice how Jo's boyfriend compares himself to Shakespeare's 'Othello'.

Throughout the play there are a number of references to the Bible, Shakespeare, classical literature and modern drama which perhaps indicate that the playwright wished to demonstrate that although the **characters** (see Literary Terms) are working class that does not mean that they are uneducated. The title of the play, taken from the *Book of Samuel* in the Bible, refers to Jonathan who tasted honey when he should not have and thus had to face punishment. It therefore suggests that each character must pay for their moments of happiness.

GLOSSARY

Mau-Mau a Kenyan political group opposed to British rule

nautical ardour sailors' passion

national service compulsory military service for men over eighteen

I was a Teenage ... one of a **genre** (see Literary Terms) of popular 1950s films, which included *I was a Teenage Werewolf* and *I was a Teenage Frankenstein*

The Ten Commandments an epic biblical blockbuster film made in 1956

Desire Under the ... Elms a play written by Eugene O'Neill

voluptuous sensuous

impotent powerless

glad rags good clothes

Lord's Day Observance Society a group in favour of maintaining Sunday as a holy day of rest

fancy bit lover

Hope Gardens an expression which meant to be overdressed

'gross clasps of the lascivious Moor' a line which describes the
undesired attentions of Othello, the black prince of
Shakespeare's play, *Othello* (Act I, Scene 1, line 127)

'Oh ill-starred wench' a reference to Desdemona, murdered by
Othello (Act V, Scene 2, line 271 of *Othello*)

Old Nick the devil

Puritan a person with strict morals

Identify the speaker.

1 'Well, we can't be together all the time and all the time there is wouldn't be enough'

2 'Honey, you've got to stop eating'

3 'I'd sooner be put on't streets. It's more honest'

4 'We're all at the steering wheel of our own destiny'

5 'Oh look at that, every line tells a dirty story, hey?'

6 'happy the corpse the rain rains on'

7 'I've done my share of suffering if I never do anymore'

Check your answers on page 61.

 Consider these issues.

a Jo's decision to stay with her boyfriend over Christmas.

b Jo's worries about madness.

c Helen's interest in Jo's boyfriend.

d Helen's criticisms of contemporary cinema, theatre and advertising.

e Jo's behaviour towards Peter.

f Attitudes towards adultery.

g The significance of the title.

h References to car and driving images.

ACT II

SCENE 1

Examine how Geof reacts to being quizzed about his sexuality.

Fairground music is heard as the scene opens. It is the following summer and Jo is visibly pregnant and living in the same flat, her Manchester maisonette. She is accompanied by Geof Ingram, an art student, who she welcomes into her flat which is still very messy. The room is in semi-darkness, which she enjoys. Geof has been thrown out of his flat so Jo offers him her 'comfortable couch' but not before she teases him about being homosexual. Jo tells Geof she works in a shoe shop during the day and a pub at night in order to maintain the flat. When Geof is persuaded to stay in her flat she confides she is pregnant and a friendly relationship develops. He is concerned for Jo and worries about finances and practical matters whereas Jo is reluctant to plan ahead. She describes herself as 'very unusual' and extraordinary, which is what her sailor boyfriend had said earlier. The two laugh and joke about themselves and end up reciting nursery rhymes and dreaming about saving the coupons which come in cigarette packets to win a car. Before falling asleep Jo sings 'Black Boy' and describes her boyfriend to Geof, praising him and calling him a Prince from darkest Africa. When Geof asks her if she still loves her sailor she protests that she is tired of love. As the pair prepare to sleep Jo speaks fondly to Geof and likens him to a 'big sister'.

The next part of the scene takes place a month or two later. It is a hot summer day as Jo complains that the flat and the whole district smell. She points out the grey coloured river and observes the dirty washing and neglected children. When she notes and criticises the mother of a particular child who she thinks is a 'bit deficient' it suggests she is worrying about the baby and her own suitability as a mother. Geof tends to domestic

Note how Geof handles Jo's threat to drown herself.

tasks, pays the rent and makes preparations for the baby's arrival by assembling clothes and organising a wicker cradle, while Jo wanders restlessly around the flat, protesting that she hates babies and wants to drown herself.

Even though Jo is generally disagreeable as her moods change constantly, Geof appears to have endless patience humouring her and trying to prepare her for motherhood. He attempts to encourage her to read a book *Looking after Baby* and ignores her teasing and taunting. When Jo asks him why he stays his reply echoes Helen's comment earlier that he does not think Jo is able to look after herself. After a brief silence, broken only by the sound of children singing outside, Geof talks to Jo about starting a relationship. Jo struggles as he kisses her and asks her to marry him. Initially he is angry and makes a racist reference about Jo's sailor boyfriend when she refuses his offer. After some plain talking Jo suggests he leaves which causes Geof to reply with striking openness that he would rather be dead than away from Jo.

Helen's unannounced entrance disturbs the peace and Jo is furious that her mother has found out about her pregnancy. Although Geof had contacted Helen he is

Notice how Helen argues that parenthood does not bring obligations.

shocked by her attitude and looks on helplessly as the two women argue, hurl insults and chase each other around the room. Eventually both Helen and Jo turn against Geof and he is ordered out of the room to make tea. When the two are calmer Helen comments about Jo looking undernourished, just as Peter did in the previous act, and places money on the table, promising more each week.

A drunk and abusive Peter then appears at the door annoyed and impatient to get to a pub. He insults everyone and, in particular, enjoys taunting Geof, calling him 'Lana', 'Mary', 'Jezebel' and an assortment of other derogatory names. He is especially aggressive towards Helen calling her a 'sour-faced old bitch' and clearly indicates that they are having marital difficulties. It seems the one thing they have in common is drinking alcohol. Peter asks Geof if he had heard of the Greek myth about Oedipus who married an older woman who turned out to be his mother which caused him to scratch out one of his eyes. Peter compares this with his own situation just before reclaiming the money Helen left on the table. Before he staggers to the bathroom Peter delights in telling them how he has been unfaithful and away from home for two weeks. Helen tries to persuade Jo to move in with her, an offer which is inevitably rejected. When Peter returns he condemns the condition of the flat and the locality and is again highly abusive to Jo and Geof. Peter declares his contempt for their social class and forces Helen to choose between him and Jo. Although she resists at first, Helen finally follows Peter and so the scene ends with Jo and Geof dancing together.

Look at what Geof says to defend the people who live in the area.

COMMENT

As someone who was homosexual in the 1950s Geoffrey Ingram would have encountered immense discrimination, for until 1957 any male homosexual act was considered an offence. The stream of cruel,

insulting comments and names directed at him by both
Peter and Helen is a clear indication of both their
contempt and society's extremely prejudiced attitude
towards homosexuality. Peter insults Geof by calling
him 'Lana', 'Mary', 'Jezebel', 'Cuddles', and 'fruitcake
parcel'. Although Jo likes Geof she teases him. She asks
prying questions about his sexuality and regularly mocks
his caring attitude towards her, calling him 'sister' and
'wife'.

Further descriptions of the neighbourhood emphasise
the dirt and poverty. Repeated comments are made
about how it smells, possibly because of its proximity to
the slaughterhouse, and yet in the background there is
the sound of children happily playing. Helen and Peter
describe the area as 'rotten' and a 'dump' although Geof
insists that the people in the district are definitely not
rotten.

GLOSSARY   spratts a type of dog biscuit
            Jack Spratt a nursery rhyme character
            his hair ... it's walking away the child has head lice
            Temperance Society a group opposed to the consumption of
              alcohol
            Oedipus a Greek king who unwittingly killed his father and
              married his mother

A *Identify the speaker.*

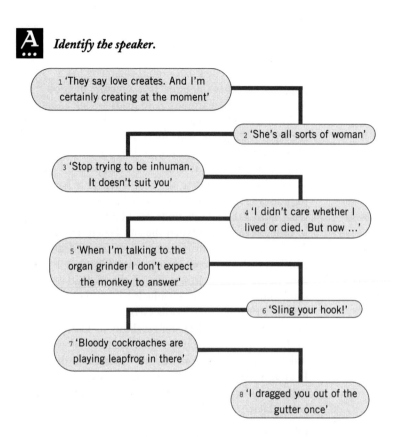

1 'They say love creates. And I'm certainly creating at the moment'

2 'She's all sorts of woman'

3 'Stop trying to be inhuman. It doesn't suit you'

4 'I didn't care whether I lived or died. But now ...'

5 'When I'm talking to the organ grinder I don't expect the monkey to answer'

6 'Sling your hook!'

7 'Bloody cockroaches are playing leapfrog in there'

8 'I dragged you out of the gutter once'

Check your answers on page 61.

B *Consider these issues.*

a Attitudes to homosexuality in the 1950s.

b The untidy, dirty conditions of the flat.

c Jo's continual inaccurate description of her boyfriend.

d Jo's repeated references to madness.

d Geof's unselfish love for Jo.

e The sometimes comical exchanges between Jo and Geof.

f The ways in which Peter reveals his marriage problems.

g Peter's comments about social class.

ACT II

SCENE 2

Jo's comment about being 'contemporary' might be linked to Shelagh Delaney's intentions of writing about contemporary issues in the play.

The final scene takes place months later as Jo's pregnancy reaches full term. It is a picture of good natured domestic harmony as Jo reads a book about childbirth and Geof cleans the flat. A discussion about the style of the book leads Jo to comment that Geof likes things to be slightly out of date. Jo is wearing a home-made housecoat which Geof compares to a badly fitting shroud. However, the couple are quite happy as Jo praises Geof for all the work he has done. When Geof moves the sofa he finds dead flower bulbs which Jo brought to the flat when she and Helen first arrived. This leads into a conversation about life and death which reveals their contrasting views. Geof has a simple view of life whereas Jo sees life as 'chaotic' and something over which individuals have little control. In a display of affection towards Geof, Jo asks him to hold her hand and talks of Helen's inability to show her love for her, describing the way Helen used to pull away in order to avoid holding Jo's hand. Throughout the scene Jo appears to be more reflective and honest about herself and her relationships even when Geof compares her to Helen.

Observing Geof moving the sofa, Jo quotes from the Bible and recalls teasing Geof when he first arrived. In return Geof playfully chases her around the flat with a mop. They remain in good spirits and Jo thanks Geof for finding her some work retouching photographs. The conversation changes to the topic of Jo's Irish ancestry and her father until Geof correctly senses that Jo has been secretly worrying about her father being 'daft'. He does his best to reassure her and suggests that Helen probably distorted the truth, but his criticisms of Helen do not prevent Jo from wishing Helen was with her as the baby's arrival is so close.

When Geof gives Jo a life-size doll to practise on, she reacts violently by throwing it on the ground protesting that it is the wrong colour and declaring she does not want to be a mother. It is at this point that for the first time she refers to her baby's father by his real name, Jimmie. She acknowledges she spent Christmas with him partly because he was gentle but mainly because she did not want to be alone yet again as she had been so often in the past. As they continue to discuss their relationship Jo states clearly that theirs is not a 'marrying' relationship. Once again Geof expresses his selfless love for Jo as he declares he is prepared to continue caring for her until she does find someone to love her. Again Jo is able to tell Geof kindly how much she appreciates his selfless affection. The two are just settling to drink tea and eat Geof's home-made cake when Helen enters, laden with luggage, talking continuously, declaring that she has arrived to take care of Jo.

Admitting the real name of her baby's father might be viewed as a sign that Jo is becoming more realistic about her situation.

Although Helen is critical of Jo, Geof and the condition of the flat she does appear to be genuinely concerned about Jo and is alarmed when she hears that Jo intends to have the baby at home rather than in hospital. Geof is prevailed upon to leave the flat briefly

so that the two women can talk. In his absence Jo
defends Geof as her only friend and insists Helen stops
insulting him. Eventually Helen is forced to admit that
her marriage to Peter is over as he has left her for a
younger woman. In a rare moment of honesty Helen is
self-critical and admits she has neglected Jo in pursuit
of her own happiness. It is at this point that Jo states
she is happy and shows she is maturing when she
declares that she feels she can take care of herself as
well as others. Unfortunately, Helen does not seem to
take much notice of Jo's comments as she immediately
starts to talk about a cot she has ordered which has pink
curtains and frills, totally unlike the wicker basket Geof
acquired. Jo is then persuaded by Helen to go for a rest
while Helen tidies the flat.

When Geof returns, Helen proceeds to criticise him,
the shopping, the condition of the flat and the wicker
basket until eventually he is forced to leave the flat
without Jo's knowledge. However, Geof's final thoughts
before departing are about Jo not himself. He tries to
persuade Helen not to frighten Jo about giving birth,
advice which is not well received by Helen. When Jo
does waken Helen avoids telling her that Geof has
gone. As they listen to the sound of children playing
outside Helen reminisces about her own childhood
singing games. It is at this point that Jo tells her mother
that her baby's father is black. Despite Jo's earlier
declaration that her mother was not colour prejudiced,
Helen is clearly shocked and even turns to the audience
for advice before exiting in search of a drink. As she
departs, Jo is left alone again, smiling and reciting the
same nursery rhyme Geof had recited when he first
arrived in the flat.

*Note the reference
Jo makes to
dreams when she
awakens.*

C OMMENT   The final scene raises questions about the past and the
future. What are Jo's prospects and will Helen return to
care for her, when in the past she has so frequently

failed in her responsibilities as a mother. Although the image of Jo reciting a nursery rhyme that Geof had sung when he first arrived may seem worrying considering the seriousness of her situation, there is other evidence which suggests that she has in fact matured.

Once Jo and Geof had settled into a routine Jo notices that Geof always seemed to be slightly out of date. Geof's reply that everyone starts life 'by living in the past' is countered by Jo's declaration that she considers herself to be 'contemporary'. This leads us to consider the significance of Jo's comment. Does she mean she is a modern, independent or unconventional young woman or is this Shelagh Delaney's view of herself?

Although Jo views life as 'chaotic', as the play draws to a close she seems to be coming to terms with the reality of her situation by confronting some of her fears and being honest about herself and her past. She talks about her childhood and Helen's failure to provide love and security, acknowledges her anxiety about inheriting her father's madness and eventually calls her sailor boyfriend by his real name. Helen is more honest in admitting some of her failings as a mother but she finds it hard to tolerate Geof and is shocked to learn Jo's baby might be black.

GLOSSARY   *Little Women* a novel by Louisa M. Alcott (1832–88) about four sisters in New England, USA

'**And he took up his bed and walked**' a quote from the Bible, Matthew 9:1–8

Ibsen's *Ghosts* a play by Henrik Ibsen, first performed in 1881

A *Identify the speaker.*

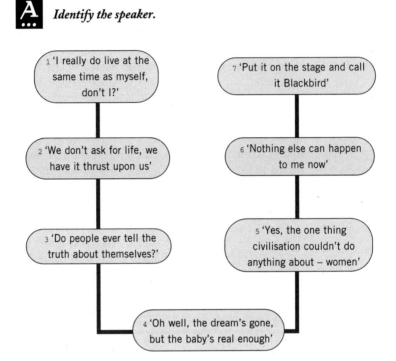

1 'I really do live at the same time as myself, don't I?'

7 'Put it on the stage and call it Blackbird'

2 'We don't ask for life, we have it thrust upon us'

6 'Nothing else can happen to me now'

3 'Do people ever tell the truth about themselves?'

5 'Yes, the one thing civilisation couldn't do anything about – women'

4 'Oh well, the dream's gone, but the baby's real enough'

Check your answers on page 61.

B *Consider these issues.*

a How Jo praises Geof.

b Jo's thoughts about death.

c The similarities between Jo and Helen.

d Geof's understanding of Jo's fears about her baby.

e How Geof accepts Jo's reasons for not wanting to marry him.

f The way Jo and Helen appear to be more relaxed and affectionate.

g The methods Helen uses to make Geof finally leave.

h Helen's reaction when Jo tells her that the baby's father is black.

PART THREE

COMMENTARY

THEMES

The central theme of *A Taste of Honey* is the relationship between a mother and daughter. As the two females struggle to overcome personal and practical difficulties and develop relationships with other **characters** (see Literary Terms), Shelagh Delaney also explores the themes of love and marriage and examines the changing nature of relationships. Although the characters appear to be resilient and cheerful as they contend with the various problems of ordinary life, recurring images of death and darkness in the play serve as a constant reminder of the harsh realities of life.

THE RELATIONSHIP BETWEEN HELEN AND JO

A Taste of Honey focuses mainly on the troubled relationship between mother and daughter and upon the lives of those who come into contact with them. Throughout the play Jo seems to be torn between wanting her mother's affection and a desire to be independent of her. At the beginning the two appear to be constantly fighting and insulting each other. Jo is understandably angered by Helen's preoccupation with herself partly because she is still quite dependent on Helen. This is demonstrated in the opening scene when Jo declares she longs to leave school, earn money and be independent of Helen, and yet when Peter arrives on the scene Jo is jealous and fights to try and prevent Helen leaving. When her mother eventually does leave the flat to marry Peter, Jo makes no effort to move from the squalid district and despite being so neglected by Helen, when Jo is almost due to give birth, she expresses a wish for Helen's company.

Notice how Jo's first job is in a pub just as Helen's first job was in a pub.

By the close of the play Helen and Jo's relationship
seems to be improving. Although they have not
resolved their differences, once Geof has left, the two
argue less and are more sensitive to each other. Jo has
become more self-reliant and less dependent even
though she is obviously pleased that Helen has
returned. Conversely, Helen has become more aware
of her deficiencies as a mother, admitting that she had
only ever thought about her own happiness not Jo's.
When Helen's marriage to Peter ends she realises she
should be with Jo and moves back to the flat,
promising support. She is openly affectionate towards
Jo, stroking her hair as she comforts her during labour
pains. However, she is so shocked when Jo tells her
that her baby will be black, she seems to revert to her
usual behaviour and leaves the flat in search of a
drink.

The title of the play was taken from the Bible and
refers to a period of happiness, a 'taste of honey', which
each **character** (see Literary Terms) experiences at
some point during the play. While Helen and Jo
develop new relationships which offer them the chance
of happiness for a short time, by the end of the play
they have both moved away from their new
relationships. Jo's boyfriend, the sailor, has disappeared,
Peter and Helen's marriage has broken up and Geof has
been forced to leave the friendship and flat he had
shared with Jo. As the play closes, Jo is left alone once
again but there is the prospect of giving birth to a new

A birth is often life and she is smiling as she remembers Geof. In fact
seen as a symbol of some feel that the essence of the play lies in what
hope. happens to Jo.

MARRIAGE AND LOVE

In the course of the play marriage is considered several
times and Helen actually weds for a second time. Helen

was divorced by her first husband because she was
unfaithful whereas her second marriage fails because of
her husband's unfaithfulness. When Jo challenges her
mother about her reasons for marrying, Helen admits
that she married the first time because she had nothing
better to do. Helen is a realist and tries to deny that
marriage is to do with romantic ideas of love and
maintains that she was attracted by Peter's money, not
love. These reasons might partly explain why Helen

Look closely at seems genuinely upset and concerned when she
how Helen reacts discovers that Jo and her boyfriend have talked about
when she discovers getting married. Once her initial anger subsides Helen
Jo has a ring from pleads with Jo to learn from her mistakes and not 'ruin'
her boyfriend. her life.

Both Peter and Jo's boyfriend talk of love when they are
Examine Peter's proposing marriage. At one point Peter sings a line
real reasons for from a popular song to explain his motive for marrying
marrying Helen. Helen, 'That wild destructive thing called love' and the
sailor claims he adores Jo even though it is obvious that
both men are mainly interested in sexual relationships.
Peter does actually marry Helen and offer her a home
and temporary financial security until he loses interest
in Helen and seeks sexual satisfaction with younger
women. The only one who displays truly unselfish love
is Geof. He provides emotional and practical support
and is prepared to stay with Jo until she finds someone
else to love her. His declaration that he would rather be
dead than parted from her conveys the strength of his
feelings. When he proposes marriage to Jo she refuses
him arguing that theirs is not a 'marrying love' because
Geof's homosexuality means he is not sexually attracted
to Jo.

DEATH AND DARKNESS

Although the play ends with the prospect of a birth,
there is a significant number of references to death and

darkness. The flat is situated close to a cemetery and a slaughterhouse. Jo brings bulbs to the flat which die and she describes a dream in which Helen's dead body is found under a rose bush. Helen compares her bed to a coffin and talks openly about the inevitability of death. As Helen prepares for her wedding, she comments about the sun shining which prompts Jo to respond, 'Yeah, and happy the corpse the rain rains on' (p. 39). During this same scene Jo learns that her 'retarded' father is dead. It is as if the references to death are meant to draw attention to the realities of life and death.

Notice Helen and Jo's contrasting thoughts about darkness.

Throughout the play there are many allusions to black, shades of darkness, the night and the absence of light. The dark is sometimes linked with the unknown, hidden and mysterious aspects of life and has both positive and negative associations. Helen and the sailor both declare they like the dark for different reasons and although Jo maintains she is afraid of the dark at the end of the first scene, she later tells Geof that she likes the half-light of Manchester evenings. Each male **character** (see Literary Terms) is in some way identified by black. Jo's boyfriend is black, Peter wears a black eye patch and Geof wears a black shirt. At some stage each one criticises the condition of the flat and its dirty location. Peter refers to the area as a 'black hole' while the sailor describes it as the 'dirtiest place' he has ever seen.

STRUCTURE

The play has an uncomplicated structure. It is divided into two acts which each contains two scenes. The action of the play evolves around Jo over a period of around nine months. Act I begins in winter just before Christmas and spans a few weeks. The second Act takes place over a period of months the following summer.

The play is set in a dilapidated flat within a deprived, industrial part of Manchester. It begins as mother and daughter enter the flat for the first time, accompanied by the sound of Jazz music and ends with Helen rushing out leaving Jo alone looking around the flat. Throughout the play music is played as characters enter and sometimes when they exit, for instance a cornet plays 'Here comes the Bride' when Helen leaves to marry Peter at the end of Act I. Scene changes are often signalled by dancing as well as music. When Jo and her boyfriend part near the beginning of Act I Scene 1, he sings to the audience as he waves goodbye while Jo and Helen dance into the next part of the scene. In the original production of the play by Joan Littlewood, the characters were each given their own individual signature tune played as the characters entered and left the stage. On a number of occasions the sounds of children playing and singing can be identified.

Frequently Peter sings lines from popular songs of the period.

As the play develops it is possible to draw certain parallels between Jo and Helen's situations. At the beginning of the play the two live together and neither appears to have a committed relationship with a man. However, within the first act, each of them becomes involved with a man who is obviously sexually attracted to them and each receives a proposal of marriage. Although Jo does not marry her boyfriend, Helen does marry Peter and leaves Jo alone in the flat. While Helen begins to build a home with Peter, Jo shares her home with Geof. By the end of the play Helen's marriage is over and so she is compelled to return to live with Jo in the flat. Unwilling to share with Geof, Helen forces him to leave. So, as the play ends mother and daughter appear to be reunited and their attitude towards each other seems to have temporarily improved. However, once Helen learns that her grandchild will be black she leaves the flat in search of a drink and Jo is left alone once again.

CHARACTERS

Jo

insecure
artistic
independent
comical
isolated

Jo is the central **character** (see Literary Terms) of the play who begins as a schoolgirl and evolves into an expectant mother. In the course of the play the action and other characters all revolve around Jo. When the play opens Jo goes to school although it is not clear how old she is for even though she tells her boyfriend she is almost eighteen she could be fifteen. Jo is eager to leave school at Christmas to earn a living partly because she has not been settled enough to become established and make any real progress in school. She eventually gets a part-time job in a pub and later as a sales assistant in a shoe shop. We learn that she has artistic ability when Helen discovers and admires some of her drawings. However, Geof, who is an art student, makes a more critical assessment of her work.

At times Jo appears to be quite an independent, strong-minded, young woman who knows what she wants in life. At other points she seems to be quite vulnerable and unable to cope. She is afraid of the darkness in houses, for instance, and she dislikes being left alone. However, these fears are quite understandable as we learn that she has frequently been left on her own and has had to learn to cope with numerous changes of address. As a result of the enforced lifestyle she appears to be isolated and lonely with few friends, a fact which is conveyed in the second act when Jo warns Helen not to insult Geof because he is her only friend (p. 79).

Jo is very critical of her mother's behaviour and failure to be a caring mother. This is conveyed from the beginning as the two women continuously argue and bicker. The way Jo addresses her mother as 'Helen' and not 'mother' suggests either that she does not respect her or that she sees herself as Helen's equal. It is apparent that Jo has often been dismissed when Helen has been entertaining men friends which accounts for her petulance and resentment when Peter visits. She also appears to be personally insecure, seeking others' opinions about her looks and comparing herself with Helen. Jo asks Peter does he 'fancy' (p. 32) her and she presses her boyfriend to say if he thinks Helen is beautiful. When she asks her boyfriend if he thinks she is like her mother, she claims to be happy when he says there is no similarity between her and Helen, just as she is angry with Geof and pulls away from him when he suggests that she is growing to be more like Helen.

Notice the number of contrasts between Helen and Jo in looks and attitudes.

Even though she is insecure at times, Jo can also be quite self-reliant and accepting. Despite being pregnant with little prospect of improving her circumstances, she seems to mature although she is definitely prone to sudden mood swings. During the period of time she shares the flat with Geof she becomes more contented, possibly because Geof offers her friendship and does not demand anything in return. Although she is not always optimistic about life which she describes as 'chaotic' (p. 71) she is capable of enjoying herself. This is most noticeable when she is laughing and joking with Geof or her boyfriend.

As her pregnancy reaches full-term, Jo talks to Geof about her fears about her baby. She also admits her feelings for Helen and talks more openly about their difficult relationship. When she tells Geof about how Helen used to refuse to hold her hand it is possible to appreciate how lonely she felt. However, a few minutes later, when she throws a doll to the ground protesting it is the wrong colour, she declares that she does not want to be a mother. Soon after the incident she listens sympathetically as Helen admits her marriage is over. Jo then talks about how she feels important and capable of taking care of everyone, including Helen.

HELEN

attractive
talkative
thoughtless
selfish
honest

Helen is an attractive looking woman who enjoys life without always thinking about her responsibilities or the consequences of her actions. Divorced from her first husband because of a brief affair with Jo's father, it is clear that she struggles to exist financially. Although it is implied that Helen gains money from men friends, Shelagh Delaney stated that Helen should not be viewed as a prostitute. Helen derives pleasure from the company of men and alcohol. In fact she depends heavily on drink, much to Jo's disapproval. When the play opens Helen is looking for a drink and at the end she leaves in search of a drink to help her get over the shock of discovering that her grandchild will be black.

Helen is obviously attractive in Peter's eyes and even Jo's boyfriend admits he thinks Helen is beautiful. Although Jo is normally Helen's harshest critic she is compelled to admit that Helen looks 'marvellous' (p. 42) as she prepares for her wedding. Helen's relationship with her daughter is a stormy one. By her own admission she has neglected Jo's emotional and physical needs: 'Have I ever laid claim to being a proper mother?' (p. 35). At times it seems she hardly knows her daughter. She seems unaware of Jo's talent for drawing, is surprised that she is afraid of the dark and is unsure if Jo has ever had a boyfriend. When she is preoccupied with Peter and other men before him, Helen completely ignores Jo, leaving her on her own for long periods of time. In fact it is only towards the close of the play that Helen admits to Jo that she realises she has often neglected her daughter in pursuit of her own happiness.

Helen sometimes reminisces about the past, remembering childhood games and songs and recalling her first job in a pub in Whit Lane. When pressed by Jo she also speaks fondly of her first love, the not very bright man who became Jo's father. But she does not dwell for too long on the past as Helen does not consider it to be wise to think about anything for too long, 'It doesn't do any good' (p. 44). She seems to simply make the most of life and accepts its realities. In the first act she reveals her down-to-earth attitude when she warns Jo to view life as 'work or want' (p. 29) and uses an image of a drunken driver at a steering wheel to convey her belief that individuals have limited control over their lives. **Ironically** (see Literary Terms) she then proceeds to inform Jo that she is about to marry Peter Smith.

Helen describes marriage as a trap.

Although she is thoughtless and selfish Helen can also be honestly self-critical and sometimes shows real concern for Jo. One significant example is when she discovers that Jo is engaged. Helen argues strongly against early marriage and pleads with Jo to learn from Helen's mistakes. Similarly, when Helen arrives at the flat after first discovering Jo is pregnant an acrimonious verbal battle develops and the two begin to chase around the flat insulting each other. When Geof intervenes Helen declares that she and Jo enjoy arguing and both of them turn against Geof. Once they are calm, Helen offers Jo money and support. This pattern of behaviour is typical of Helen who is a changeable character. She can be kind and caring just as she can be cruel and insulting. She is so resentful of Geof that she cannot rest until she has insulted and intimidated him so much that he leaves the flat. Conversely, Helen is gentle and supportive of Jo when her labour pains begin.

GEOF

supportive
sensitive
considerate
selfless
patient

Geof is a young art student who offers Jo considerable practical support and friendship. He is a caring, intelligent individual who is sensitive to Jo's feelings and fears and tolerant of her mood swings. When he first enters the flat, he is homeless, evicted from his flat possibly because of his homosexuality. During the play he has to put up with taunts about his sexuality from Jo and endure insults and abuse from Helen and Peter.

It is Geof who tidies and cleans the flat, does the shopping, pays the rent from his grant and secures work for Jo retouching photographs. He also works hard at trying to prepare Jo for her baby's arrival by making clothes, securing a wicker-basket cot and buying a book for Jo about childbirth.

Geof and Jo are happy and contented most of the time. They laugh and joke and sing nursery rhymes to each other. Geof's feelings for Jo are very strong. Although he is not sexually attracted to Jo, Geof offers to marry her. When he is refused he reveals the depth of his selfless love for her by declaring he would rather be dead than separated from her. He puts Jo's needs before his own, announcing he will stay with her until she finds the right person to love. Jo compares Geof to a sister because he makes her feel secure and does not make emotional or sexual demands.

It is Geof who contacts Helen as he feels Jo needs her and in the end he makes the decision to leave because he cares for Jo and knows that she cannot deal with the tension between him and Helen. Although he is unhappy about having to leave Jo his first concern is for her happiness which prompts him to warn Helen not to frighten her.

PETER

Peter Smith is described as a brash salesman who wears an eye-patch and smokes cigars. He is at least ten years younger than Helen and appears to be successful at making money. He drives, purchases a house and

ambitious
wealthy
unfaithful
generous
aggressive

spends his money freely, buying gifts for Helen and chocolates for Jo. Clearly he is ambitious and makes it plain that he detests the place where Helen and Jo live.

He is initially infatuated with Helen and takes no interest in Jo although he does concede to answer a barrage of some very personal questions which she fires at him. It is at this point he explains that he wears an eye-patch because he lost an eye during the war. In the first act Peter plays the part of the persistent lover who ignores Helen's rebuffs in an effort to persuade her to join him for a drink. In fact both Helen and Peter enjoy drinking heavily. Peter incorporates lines from popular songs into his conversations particularly when trying to persuade Helen to marry him. He likes to boast of his good-looks and prospects and declares he prefers older women in an effort to win Helen's attention.

In the second act Peter is less impressed with Helen and appears on stage as an aggressive drunk. He still sings lines from popular tunes and hurls abusive comments at everyone as he staggers about the flat demanding that Helen leaves with him. By this stage he is comparing himself to Oedipus who married his mother by mistake. He also openly boasts of his marital infidelities so that it is not a surprise at the end of the play to learn that his marriage to Helen is over because he has gone off with another woman.

THE BOY   Jo's boyfriend , the father of her baby, is a black, twenty-two-year-old sailor from Cardiff in Wales who used to be a nurse before commencing his national service. Although he only appears twice in the play he is not properly identified by his real name until the end of the second act when Jo calls him Jimmie. In the script he is called 'Boy'. Jo refers to him as her 'black prince' and 'Prince Ossini' whilst he compares himself to Othello.

gentle
amusing
amorous
intelligent
caring

Jo says she was attracted to him because he could sing and was gentle. He is obviously interested in Jo and tells her he loves her and offers to marry her. From the start it is clear that he experiences racial prejudice because he expresses surprise that Jo is not ashamed to be seen with him in public. He also anticipates a negative reaction from Jo's mother when their engagement is announced. However, he is a light-hearted character who laughs and jokes with Jo and admits he cannot see her in the evening because he intends to go drinking with his friends.

When he goes to Jo's flat he expresses his dislike of the dirty location but he is prepared to take care of Jo for the short time they are together. He makes Jo a cold cure and happily accepts her invitation to stay with her over Christmas although he is honest, making his intentions plain and telling Jo he is sexually experienced. Despite the marriage proposal, the sailor disappears from Jo's life. But during their brief relationship he had provided Jo with a little tenderness, a brief taste of happiness which she so desperately needed.

LANGUAGE AND STYLE

When Shelagh Delaney set out to write *A Taste of Honey* her aim was to write as people talk. Clearly she achieved her aim for the language that her **characters** (see Literary Terms) use in the play is the language of those she heard around her: the language of ordinary working-class people.

Although the characters in *A Taste of Honey* live in the north of England and may be represented by actors as having regional accents, there are few indications in the text of a regional dialect. There is a very limited number of Lancashire expressions and non-standard features of language included in the play. One example is when Helen says 'Eee' as she shivers with cold in the first scene. Also, at one point Jo drops letters and says 'on't street' instead of 'on the street'. Although the vocabulary used by all the characters is varied there are a few examples of dialect. Children play on the 'croft' which is dialect for a piece of waste land and Helen recalls a 'Clough' which describes a ravine or gorge. Apart from a few such examples the characters all speak fluent Standard English.

All the characters are articulate and engage in lively, fast-moving conversations. Short sentences and quick, witty comments are characteristics of the **dialogue** (see Literary Terms). The characters have a tendency to jump from one subject to another in the middle of a speech which shows how Shelagh Delaney effectively managed to capture the way in which people actually speak. There are numerous occasions when the characters appear to be not speaking directly to the other person but to a third party, possibly the audience. This is particularly noticeable in the first scene as Helen and Jo argue and criticise each other. When Helen cannot find a glass, Jo snaps 'You packed 'em. She'd lose her head if it was loose'.

Peter frequently incorporates the lyrics of popular songs into his conversations which gives a sense of the period. Derogatory labels and names are used regularly. Jo calls the landlady an 'old mare' (p. 55) while Peter calls Helen 'a game old bird' (p. 66). Jo is called a slut and a whore by Peter and Helen once they know she is pregnant and a torrent of abusive terms are aimed at Geof who is labelled a 'freak' because of his homosexuality. There are instances of swearing although they tend to be confined to those scenes where characters are either drunk or in conflict. Peter is perhaps the most coarse and aggressive character particularly in Act II when in his role as comic drunk he is verbally abusive to everyone and falls around the flat.

Despite the serious themes of the play much of the **dialogue** (see Literary Terms) and action is comical. In the opening scene Jo and Helen are like sparring partners as Jo deflates Helen's exaggerations through sarcasm and criticism. This is further highlighted in the second act when Helen first comes to offer help to Jo. A quarrel quickly develops and the two females begin to chase around the flat as Geof attempts to intervene. Eventually Geof yells at them to stop shouting just as they have momentarily fallen silent. Comedy sometimes arises through the characters' actions, such as when Jo attacks Peter to try and prevent him dating Helen or when in the second act Peter falls into the kitchen, but most of the comic elements come through the dialogue of the quarrels and confrontations.

Notice the fast-moving banter between Jo, Helen and Peter which begins as soon as Peter enters.

PART FOUR

STUDY SKILLS

HOW TO USE QUOTATIONS

One of the secrets of success in writing essays is the way you use quotations. There are five basic principles:

- Put inverted commas at the beginning and end of the quotation
- Write the quotation exactly as it appears in the original
- Do not use a quotation that repeats what you have just written
- Use the quotation so that it fits into your sentence
- Keep the quotation as short as possible

Quotations should be used to develop the line of thought in your essays.

Your comment should not duplicate what is in your quotation. For example:

Geof asks Helen not to frighten Jo, 'I said would you not frighten Jo' (p. 83).

Far more effective is to write:

Geof tells Helen not to 'frighten Jo'.

Always lay out the lines as they appear in the text. For example:

Helen is shocked by the news of Jo's pregnancy:
'Oh yes … I don't know what's to be done with you, I don't really.'

However, the most sophisticated way of using the writer's words is to embed them into your sentence:

Jo criticises her mother for being 'a real fool'.

When you use quotations in this way, you are demonstrating the ability to use text as evidence to support your ideas - not simply including words from the original to prove you have read it.

Everyone writes differently. Work through the suggestions given here and adapt the advice to suit your own style and interests. This will improve your essay-writing skills and allow your personal voice to emerge.

The following points indicate in ascending order the skills of essay writing:
- Picking out one or two facts about the story and adding the odd detail
- Writing about the text by retelling the story
- Retelling the story and adding a quotation here and there
- Organising an answer which explains what is happening in the text and giving quotations to support what you write

....

- Writing in such a way as to show that you have thought about the intentions of the writer of the text and that you understand the techniques used
- Writing at some length, giving your viewpoint on the text and commenting by picking out details to support your views
- Looking at the text as a work of art, demonstrating clear critical judgement and explaining to the reader of your essay how the enjoyment of the text is assisted by literary devices, linguistic effects and psychological insights; showing how the text relates to the time when it was written

The dotted line above represents the division between lower and higher level grades. Higher-level performance begins when you start to consider your response as a reader of the text. The highest level is reached when you offer an enthusiastic personal response and show how this piece of literature is a product of its time.

Coursework essay

Set aside an hour or so at the start of your work to plan what you have to do.

- List all the points you feel are needed to cover the task. Collect page references of information and quotations that will support what you have to say. A helpful tool is the highlighter pen: this saves painstaking copying and enables you to target precisely what you want to use.

- Focus on what you consider to be the main points of the essay. Try to sum up your argument in a single sentence, which could be the closing sentence of your essay. Depending on the essay title, it could be a statement about a character: Geof's actions demonstrate his genuine concern for Jo; an opinion about language: Peter's use of abusive language shows his contempt for Geof, Jo and Helen; or a judgement on a theme: in the end Helen and Jo are alone without the men who proposed marriage.

- Make a short essay plan. Use the first paragraph to introduce the argument you wish to make. In the following paragraphs develop this argument with details, examples and other possible points of view. Sum up your argument in the last paragraph. Check you have answered the question.

- Write the essay, remembering all the time the central point you are making.

- On completion, go back over what you have written to eliminate careless errors and improve expression. Read it aloud to yourself, or, if you are feeling more confident, to a relative or friend.

If you can, try to type your essay, using a word processor. This will allow you to correct and improve your writing without spoiling its appearance.

Examination essay

The essay written in an examination often carries more marks than the coursework essay even though it is written under considerable time pressure.

In the revision period build up notes on various aspects of the text you are using. Fortunately, in acquiring this set of York Notes on *A Taste of Honey,* you have made a prudent beginning! York Notes are set out to give you vital information and help you to construct your personal overview of the text.

Make notes with appropriate quotations about the key issues of the set text. Go into the examination knowing your text and having a clear set of opinions about it.

In most English Literature examinations you can take in copies of your set books. This in an enormous advantage although it may lull you into a false sense of security. Beware! There is simply not enough time in an examination to read the book from scratch.

In the examination

- Read the question paper carefully and remind yourself what you have to do.
- Look at the questions on your set texts to select the one that most interests you and mentally work out the points you wish to stress.
- Remind yourself of the time available and how you are going to use it.
- Briefly map out a short plan in note form that will keep your writing on track and illustrate the key argument you want to make.
- Then set about writing it.
- When you have finished, check through to eliminate errors.

To summarise, these are the keys to success:

- **Know the text**
- **Have a clear understanding of and opinions on the storyline, characters, setting, themes and writer's concerns**
- **Select the right material**
- **Plan and write a clear response, continually bearing the question in mind**

A typical essay question on *A Taste of Honey* is followed by a sample essay plan in note form. You will need to look back through the text to find quotations to support your points. Think about your own ideas – the sample answer is only a suggestion and you may wish to ignore it and produce your own. But it is always a good idea to plan out your thoughts first – it will save you time and help you to organise your ideas. Remember – try to answer the question!

From dependence to independence. To what degree does Jo mature and become less dependent on others?

Introduction
- Begin with a brief description of Jo's character at the end and the beginning of the play
- To what extent is she dependent upon others at the start and finish
- Does she seek attention and affection?

Part 1
- Describe Jo in Act I and note her abilities, schooling and interests
- What is her reaction to the flat?
- Consider her attitudes to life and frequent moves
- Is she lonely?

Part 2
- Examine her relationship with Helen
- Discuss the way they communicate
- Note how Jo criticises Helen and does not call her 'mother'

Part 3
- Describe Jo's reaction and behaviour towards Peter
- Consider her fear of the dark and being alone
- Are her needs considered?
- Is she independent for her age?

Part 4
- Consider her relationship with the sailor
- What comfort does he offer?
- Does she love him or expect him to return?
- Do her ideas about him change?

SAMPLE ESSAY PLAN continued

Part 5
- Examine her friendship with Geof
- Compare Geof and the sailor
- How does Jo behave towards Geof?

Part 6
- Note how Jo starts to mature and value Geof
- Discuss whether she becomes more realistic about her baby, her mother and the future
- Is she ready for motherhood?

Conclusion
- Return to the title focus and decide if there are signs that Jo has matured and is capable of living independently

FURTHER QUESTIONS

The following questions require a knowledge of the whole play. You should make a plan like the one on the previous pages before attempting any of the essays.

1 To what degree are the issues of the play relevant to contemporary society?
2 Discuss whether or not Helen deserves to be called a bad mother.
3 Compare and contrast the different attitudes towards women demonstrated by Peter, Geof and the sailor.
4 Consider the various forms of love presented in the play.
5 To what degree do the main characters have control over their own lives? Do they make free choices or are they victims of their own destiny?
6 Describe the relationship between Helen and Jo and discuss how it develops.
7 To what degree is *A Taste of Honey* a play about social class and inequalities?
8 Examine Geof's significance in the play.

9 The importance of parenthood is a central theme of
  A Taste of Honey. How does Delaney convey her
  ideas on the theme?

10 Discuss the comic elements in the play.

PART FIVE

CULTURAL CONNECTIONS

BROADER PERSPECTIVES

Absurd drama   When Shelagh Delaney wrote *A Taste of Honey* she intended to produce a drama which would convey a realistic picture of contemporary life in 1950s Britain. It was written as a reaction to the mainstream plays of the post-war period which tended to be fairly traditional, either dramas about the upper classes or drawing room comedies. Delaney was one of the new playwrights who were beginning to emerge and who were developing two types of theatre, 'the absurd' and 'social drama'. The term 'absurd' was first used to describe drama which represented life as meaningless, a classic example of this genre being Samuel Beckett's *Waiting for Godot* (1953).

Social drama   Social drama was introduced by a younger generation of playwrights frequently from the working classes. Perhaps the most significant writer was John Osborne who wrote *Look Back in Anger*, which was staged at the Royal Court Theatre, London in 1956. The hero of this play was Jimmy Porter, the original 'angry young man' who represented the concerns of the younger generation demanding changes in society. *A Taste of Honey* had a similarly immediate impact. The introduction of a working-class female **protagonist** (see Literary Terms) who had a homosexual companion and an interracial relationship was controversial and led critics to group Shelagh Delaney with Osborne and his contemporaries.

Kitchen-sink drama   Another successful playwright of the time was Arnold Wesker whose plays, *The Wesker Trilogy* (1958–60) and *The Kitchen* (1959), gave rise to another term, 'kitchen-sink' drama. This term referred to the use of family and domestic settings in dramas to examine social and class issues. *A Taste of Honey* was hailed as a kitchen-sink drama in that it portrayed the lives of a group working-class people, living in a deprived, inner-city environment, struggling to overcome practical problems and personal conflicts. However, the play's humour and, some will argue, its underlying sense of optimism are factors which, according to some critics, prevent it from being placed within this genre.

A film version of *A Taste of Honey*, made in 1961, starring Rita Tushingham as Jo and Dora Bryan as Helen, won a BAFTA award for best picture. It was described in a Halliwell's film guide as a fascinating, off-beat comedy. It is also performed regularly by theatre groups so watch out for local productions.

LITERARY TERMS

atmosphere the mood which dominates a scene

character the person invented in a text

colloquialisms expressions used in everyday speech rather than formal language

context the surrounding ideas, setting or words which give meaning

dialogue the conversation which takes place between characters

genre the type of literature. The major genres within literature are poetry, prose (novels) and drama. They can be further subdivided into genre. Novels may be romances, ghost or horror stories for instance

irony saying one thing whilst meaning another

melodrama used to describe situations which are over dramatic or improbable

protagonist this usually means the main character or actor in a play

TEST ANSWERS

TEST YOURSELF (Act I Scene 1)

A
1 Peter
2 Helen
3 Helen
4 Jo
5 Jo
6 Peter
7 Helen

TEST YOURSELF (Act II Scene 1)

A
1 Jo
2 Jo
3 Geof
4 Geof
5 Helen
6 Helen
7 Peter
8 Peter

TEST YOURSELF (Act I Scene 2)

A
1 Jo
2 Boy
3 Jo
4 Helen
5 Helen
6 Jo
7 Helen

TEST YOURSELF (Act II Scene 2)

A
1 Jo
2 Jo
3 Geof
4 Geof
5 Geof
6 Helen
7 Helen

NOTES

GCSE and equivalent levels (£3.50 each)

Maya Angelou
I Know Why the Caged Bird Sings

Jane Austen
Pride and Prejudice

Alan Ayckbourn
Absent Friends

Elizabeth Barrett Browning
Selected Poems

Robert Bolt
A Man for All Seasons

Harold Brighouse
Hobson's Choice

Charlotte Brontë
Jane Eyre

Emily Brontë
Wuthering Heights

Shelagh Delaney
A Taste of Honey

Charles Dickens
David Copperfield

Charles Dickens
Great Expectations

Charles Dickens
Hard Times

Charles Dickens
Oliver Twist

Roddy Doyle
Paddy Clarke Ha Ha Ha

George Eliot
Silas Marner

George Eliot
The Mill on the Floss

William Golding
Lord of the Flies

Oliver Goldsmith
She Stoops To Conquer

Willis Hall
The Long and the Short and the Tall

Thomas Hardy
Far from the Madding Crowd

Thomas Hardy
The Mayor of Casterbridge

Thomas Hardy
Tess of the d'Urbervilles

Thomas Hardy
The Withered Arm and other Wessex Tales

L.P. Hartley
The Go-Between

Seamus Heaney
Selected Poems

Susan Hill
I'm the King of the Castle

Barry Hines
A Kestrel for a Knave

Louise Lawrence
Children of the Dust

Harper Lee
To Kill a Mockingbird

Laurie Lee
Cider with Rosie

Arthur Miller
The Crucible

Arthur Miller
A View from the Bridge

Robert O'Brien
Z for Zachariah

Frank O'Connor
My Oedipus Complex and other stories

George Orwell
Animal Farm

J.B. Priestley
An Inspector Calls

Willy Russell
Educating Rita

Willy Russell
Our Day Out

J.D. Salinger
The Catcher in the Rye

William Shakespeare
Henry IV Part 1

William Shakespeare
Henry V

William Shakespeare
Julius Caesar

William Shakespeare
Macbeth

William Shakespeare
The Merchant of Venice

William Shakespeare
A Midsummer Night's Dream

William Shakespeare
Much Ado About Nothing

William Shakespeare
Romeo and Juliet

William Shakespeare
The Tempest

William Shakespeare
Twelfth Night

George Bernard Shaw
Pygmalion

Mary Shelley
Frankenstein

R.C. Sherriff
Journey's End

Rukshana Smith
Salt on the snow

John Steinbeck
Of Mice and Men

Robert Louis Stevenson
Dr Jekyll and Mr Hyde

Jonathan Swift
Gulliver's Travels

Robert Swindells
Daz 4 Zoe

Mildred D. Taylor
Roll of Thunder, Hear My Cry

Mark Twain
Huckleberry Finn

James Watson
Talking in Whispers

William Wordsworth
Selected Poems

A Choice of Poets

Mystery Stories of the Nineteenth Century including The Signalman

Nineteenth Century Short Stories

Poetry of the First World War

Six Women Poets

York Notes Advanced (£3.99 each)

Margaret Atwood
The Handmaid's Tale

Jane Austen
Mansfield Park

Jane Austen
Persuasion

Jane Austen
Pride and Prejudice

Alan Bennett
Talking Heads

William Blake
Songs of Innocence and of Experience

Charlotte Brontë
Jane Eyre

Emily Brontë
Wuthering Heights

Geoffrey Chaucer
The Franklin's Tale

Geoffrey Chaucer
General Prologue to the Canterbury Tales

Geoffrey Chaucer
The Wife of Bath's Prologue and Tale

Joseph Conrad
Heart of Darkness

Charles Dickens
Great Expectations

John Donne
Selected Poems

George Eliot
The Mill on the Floss

F. Scott Fitzgerald
The Great Gatsby

E.M. Forster
A Passage to India

Brian Friel
Translations

Thomas Hardy
The Mayor of Casterbridge

Thomas Hardy
Tess of the d'Urbervilles

Seamus Heaney
Selected Poems from Opened Ground

Nathaniel Hawthorne
The Scarlet Letter

James Joyce
Dubliners

John Keats
Selected Poems

Christopher Marlowe
Doctor Faustus

Arthur Miller
Death of a Salesman

Toni Morrison
Beloved

William Shakespeare
Antony and Cleopatra

William Shakespeare
As You Like It

William Shakespeare
Hamlet

William Shakespeare
King Lear

William Shakespeare
Measure for Measure

William Shakespeare
The Merchant of Venice

William Shakespeare
Much Ado About Nothing

William Shakespeare
Othello

William Shakespeare
Romeo and Juliet

William Shakespeare
The Tempest

William Shakespeare
The Winter's Tale

Mary Shelley
Frankenstein

Alice Walker
The Color Purple

Oscar Wilde
The Importance of Being Earnest

Tennessee Williams
A Streetcar Named Desire

John Webster
The Duchess of Malfi

W.B. Yeats
Selected Poems